bowls

THE BOWLS DICTIONARY

British Library Cataloguing in Publication Data

Dunstan, Keith
The lawn bowls dictionary.
1. Bowling on the green—Anecdotes, facetiae, satire, etc.
I. Title
796.31 GV909

ISBN 0-7153-9041-4

First published in Australia by Sun Books 1986
First published in Great Britain by David & Charles 1987

Printed in Hong Kong
for David & Charles Publishers plc
Brunel House Newton Abbot Devon

bowls

THE BOWLS DICTIONARY
BY KEITH DUNSTAN
ILLUSTRATED BY JEFF HOOK

DAVID & CHARLES
Newton Abbot London

Absolute...
4

A

Absolute	A bowl which rolls over and actually nestles up to kitty almost in an embrace. Very tiresome when perpetrated by your opponent.
Age	Age? What's that? This is a sport which caters for fourteen-year-olds as well as crafty characters in the nineties. Some come into the game when their speed and stamina begin to fail at lesser and more sweaty sports. But skill is not bound up with years. Bowls is a game for all seasons and your age is a bother only when you admit it to yourself.
Amateur	One who doesn't shout in the bar.
Anxiety	Wondering: • If your bra is about to break. • If you left the oven on. • If you go into the low crouch whether you'll ever get up again. • If in your hurry you have just put on the wrong bias. • And what Dad will say when you tell him that when you play bowls it's only take-away pizza for dinner.
Associate	Vintage term for lady bowler. Don't use it—that's if you want to survive till dinner time.
Autumn	The grass at the north-south ends of the rink has worn thin and has acquired a suntan. Fred, the groundsman, is finding it harder and harder to iron out the pockmarks and he has ordered soil for winter top dressing. But it is a sublime time of the year. There is a

gentleness, a mellowness in the air. The sunny, windless days are so gorgeous they could have been designed by a computer. Just like life itself, nature in autumn is not quite so contrary or desperate.

B

Baby — This describes an end in which the jack has been bowled to a desperately short distance. It is not a sexist term which one uses to address the cute female bowler on the next rink.

Back — Totally contrary device composed of 5500 bones, discs and hunks of decaying tissue, designed to keep doctors, chiropractors, nurses and physiotherapists in eternal prosperity.

Backhand — When all else fails, you come round the other way and try the backhand. Like your backhand in tennis, it suffers terribly from lack of use. Actually, your backhand is also the hand you use to rub your ailing back.

Backspin — Step back, admire the beauty of the head-work, tread on a bowl and it is no trouble at all.

Backswing — It is the same in all sports: tennis, golf, hockey, baseball, cricket, even football. The whole secret is in the graceful backswing and the perfect follow-through. If only you could put it in the right direction.

Back (see also Backhand)...

Bankers...

Bag	There is a certain upmanship in having the right, beautifully-crafted bag. It can carry your purse, your comb, lipstick, nail file and . . . oh yes . . . measure, polishing cloth, polished and perfectly matched bowls.
Ball	Unquestionably bowls is the most ancient and distinguished of ball games. There is a theory that Adam was the first bowler when he bowled rocks along the ground. Naturally Eve was the first associate. The rules about dress didn't come until later.
Bank	Raised ground beyond the ditch. Useful insurance to prevent the maiming of spectators.
Bankers	Spectators who occupy the bank. Like sidewalk superintendents who gather on building sites, they believe they know more than the people doing the job.
Beer	Much easier to draw than a jack.
Beginner	That's what he tells you, then knocks you off 21 to nil.
Bending	It has been said there is not much exercise associated with bowls. This is uttered by people who have never played the game. Have you ever noticed how much bending is required? The great cricketer, Keith Miller, could flick the ball into his hand with his toes. Bowls are too heavy for that. But you *can* buy an ingenious wire device, which is the perfect picker-upper.
Be Up	Plaintive cry almost as evocative and heart-rending as 'Howzat' in cricket. Someone is always urging you to be 'Be up', to get up there on target. It is an evocative, plaintive cry at home too. But anyone can 'be up' on bowls mornings.

Bias	You never deviate. Your absolute preference every time in the mixed bowls is your devoted wife. (*See* Wrong Bias.)
Blazer	The quality of the bowling arm is in inverse proportion to the brilliance of the cut and the dazzling newness of the blazer.
Block Shot	There is very little that will stop a bowler from playing bowls. You can take the battery out of the car. That helps.
Body Language	Many believe it is possible to turn your bowl by sheer will power. There are various methods. You can stand on one foot, you can shift your bottom to the left or the right, or you can do a Nureyev *entrechat*. It is known as body language.
Bowl	Device created with extraordinary scientific precision never to go in the direction required—with the object of torturing the creature who plays with it.
Bowler	Creature who tires easily at home. Particularly weakened by the sight of a vacuum cleaner, rake, broom or paint brush, but who, amazingly enough, can put in ten hours on a bowling green without any sign of fatigue.
Bowling Alley	Game invented for making use of old movie theatres.
Bowls	Mysterious and ancient game played by people old enough to know better, using balls carefully designed to go in the wrong direction.

Body Language...

Bumps...

Breaking Point	This is the point when the bowl begins to slow and takes on a generous curve. We usually find it comes about 8 pm, when you haven't telephoned that you'll be late for dinner.
Bumps	Of course, they are supposed to be dead level. Local knowledge is knowing all the little alpine sections of the track, all the little hollows. Nothing like a few bumps to bring a visiting champion down to earth.

C

Cake	Frequently the jack is called 'the cake', because it gets into so many indigestible positions.
Chalk	Material for writing loving messages on bowls when they have been deeply touched.
Changing Ends	Something you are always doing in bowls. You change ends as often as they do in tennis. It is a time for wistful meditation and as you pass your opponents you try to smile benignly, even though they have you down 20 to nil.
Claw	Classic bowls grip. Used particularly by the secretary when collecting club subscriptions.
Clinic	In the old days you just had instructions from a friend, or you would get tips from the skip in his spare moments. Now they run bowling week-ends at the country club and there is a clinic. The only trouble is Medicare doesn't pay the bills.

Changing End...

Colour...

Club	Band of happy, social people worrying how they can get by without again raising the subscription.
Colour	Dangerous, disturbing ingredient, not allowed in dress. Permitted only on cheeks, lips, noses and television.
Committee	Group which usually only agrees on the time to go home.
Compaction	The green is hard, unyielding, suffering from over-work. Now badly in deed of aeration. The feeling in your feet is exactly likewise.
Compassion	Members have been known to carry bags for old ladies but on the rinks it hasn't been seen since the days of Sir Francis Drake.
Concentration	Champions now 'psych' themselves before the game. Absolute concentration on the bowl is deemed essential. All extraneous thoughts must be driven from the mind. Thoughts most difficult to remove are believed to be these: • What's on for dinner. • Sex. • A glass of something good with ice tinkling against the side. • Sex. • Money and how to pay the rates bill. • Sex.

Concentration...
8

Crack an Egg...

Conversation	Males: 20 per cent bowls, 20 per cent weather, 20 per cent sex, 10 per cent booze, 20 per cent things aren't as good as they used to be, 10 per cent this Government will ruin us. Females: 30 per cent bowls, 10 per cent weather, 20 per cent clothes and cooking, 30 per cent children and grandchildren, 9 per cent things aren't as good as they used to be, 1 per cent men.
Crack an Egg	When you nudge out an opponent's bowl with all the delicacy of a maiden's first kiss, my goodness, you *have* cracked an egg.
Cricket Pitch	When you send down the jack to the minimum length according to the rules, it is sometimes called a 'cricket pitch', a term derived from a less exciting, junior sport.
Critics	They sit in tiered seats along the side of the green. Put them together male and female and you have 10,000 years of extraordinary wisdom and experience. Verdict: The standard was immeasurably better 20 years ago.
Crouch	You go down into the crouch or the semi-crouch. Perhaps only at Mass is there so much going down on one's knees. Genuine prayer is a help on both occasions.
Curves	Oh yes, you do get curves on bowling greens but most of them are rather more generous than they were 25 years ago.

D

Dead Bowl	That's how you feel next day.
Delivery	You don't heave, chuck, throw, toss or even trundle. You deliver the wood. It is very nearly the only hand delivery left.
Diet	There are books now on proper diets for bowlers. They tell you to lay off heavy food six hours before bowling. They advise against red meat, fatty foods, sugar, salt, caffein, white flour and, oh dear, even beer. They tell you you've got to have fibre, you've got to drink six glasses of water a day. You can have a heart attack worrying about it all.
Disc	In the old days bowls always had a disc of ivory or metal on both sides to distinguish one bowl from another. Now, in this plastic era, sometimes there is a design instead. The biased side has a smaller disc, and should be very carefully noted every time, one hopes.
Discrimination	Males can wear brown or black shoes. Women can wear only white. Women must wear skirts of a certain length. Males can wear long trousers or shorts. It's tradition. A woman in shorts and brown shoes would be a bigger shock than a topless player at Wimbledon.
Ditch	The tragic thing about bowls is one always ends up in the ditch.
Doubles	The ultimate calorific sin, and you hope nobody is looking—a double header at the American ice cream shop on the way home.

Disc...
10

Dress...

Draw	This is the basic shot in bowls. The object is to send your bowl up the green so that it cuddles sweetly up to your target. You know how it is. Some days you are drawing better than Michelangelo. Other days you couldn't draw a beer.
Dress	The rest of the world has gone to ruin in a hideous sea of denim. Tennis players dress like trendies at a beach party. Cricketers turn out in pyjamas. Bowlers remain the last secure stronghold of virgin white. Indeed a group of female bowlers on a bus stop could be a covey of nuns. Although, it is said, their conversation in the wash room tends to be slightly different.
Duke of Suffolk	Bowls is the one sport where bent behaviour is compulsory. Legend has it that bias began with the Duke of Suffolk in 1522. His Grace was playing at Goole, Yorkshire, when he split his bowl in two. He dashed inside, sawed a wooden ball off the top of the bannisters and went on with the game. Naturally the bowl had a flat bottom and rolled off kilter in a delightful curve. The Duke was able to get round his opponents and he won four ends in succession. Nobody could stop bias after that.
Dumper	Lack of smooth delivery and dropping the bowl on the green. Best done out of sight of the greenkeeper. Usually caused by having your bottom insufficiently close to the turf.

Dumper...

Equal Opportunity...

E

Ends	You have ends. You deliver your four bowls up one way, then you deliver them down in the opposite direction. That's so you can never be sure of the wind or what you are doing. The means have to justify the ends.
Equal Opportunity	Allowing females inside and letting them put their feet on the brass rail.
Euggghhhhh	Enthusiastic comment when your drive misses its target by a full metre, jumps the ditch, clears the bank and ends up in the members' car park.
Exquisite self-restraint	You have played the shot of the year. Exactly according to the skip's instructions with utmost delicacy you have weaved through two, narrowly separated woods delicately to touch the kitty. Bosisto himself would have been proud. Then their number three sends down a blistering drive which blasts you into the ditch. Instead of mouthing McEnroe obscenities your sweet loving nature says: 'What a beautiful shot'.

F

Fanatic	One who tries to fit in sleep between bowling.
Feet	Your back's not too good. Your neck gets stiff after six ends. There's the pain in your right elbow and you

Fanatic ...

Female Bowler...

	could do with a new pair of knees, but ultimately it's the feet that go. It'd be nice to be up in Heaven if you could play bowls in bare feet.
Female Bowler	An awesome creature. Her fanaticism transcends even that of the bridge player. The disease is said to be terminal, if she could she would play six days a week. Don't expect dinner on bowling days, a take-away is the only hope. When she comes home it will take an hour to tell of the brilliance of her plays. But don't think it has all just begun. Anne Boleyn was a pretty good bowler. That's until they removed her head.
Fête	The one worse than death that you fear might be necessary to raise money for the club house extensions.
Flukes	Other people have flukes. Yours are always brilliant ideas skilfully carried into execution.
Forehand	Overworked hand used for shaking hands with opponents and umpires, receiving trophies and, most of all, paying out losing bets.
Foot Fault	The fellow who turned out in awful joggers with stripes down the side.
Four Play	Still indulged in, quite regardless of age.
Führer	Kindly name for the club president.
Funeral	There is the classic story of the bowler who lifted his hat just as he was about to make a delivery. The other bowlers looked askance, but then they forgave him this lapse in concentration. The funeral of his late wife was just passing by.

G

Gallopers	Creatures who gallop after their play. They cajole, entreat, gesticulate, wave and dance. You being a well-mannered, reserved individual would never do that. You quietly walk down the rink . . . and *pray* that the little _ _ _ _ _ _ _ _ will go in the right direction.
Gardening	Pastime carried out by non-bowlers.
Good Loser	A skill you acquire with lots of practice.
Grand Final Day	Day of glorious peace when sanity returns to the land and the scourge of football is over. Time when it is possible to find partners again for a civilised, non-barbarous activity.
Grass	Inefficient material invented by God to provide splendid employment for large teams of ground staff.
Grassing	The act of getting the bowl out of your hand on to the turf. Gravity will handle it, no trouble at all, but there are about 2750 books to tell you how to do it properly.
Grass Line	Of course the damn thing curves, so you have to decide how far out from the centre line you bowl. This is your grass line. You 'take' grass, thank-you very much, and having taken grass with superb judgement, nestling within two millimetres of the kitty, the blighter knocks you into the dish with his next bowl.
Green Director	Old Fred has been on the job here for 35 years and inherited it from his father. He understands the mysteries of water weed, dollar spot, how to eradicate the evils of paspalum. He is a law unto himself if he

Gallopers...

Grip...

	decides rink four is to be rested and nobody will tell him when it's time to bring out the spikes and aerate the soil. And he's crafty. Some say that when the English arrive, with their love of slow greens, he turns on a track faster than the Indiannapolis Speedway.
Grip	There are three major grips: the claw, the cradle and the finger. The cradle is popular in England where they still have the noble belief that the hand which uses the cradle rules the world.

H

Hat	Charming, formal, historic device still worn by generals, policemen, bishops, bank robbers and bowlers.
Head	As they say, this is where it's all at: the jack and the live bowls around it. You can have a good head, a bad head, an elegant head, an untidy head and it is important always before playing your wood to examine heads. A good head specialist is really a psychiatrist. Then, of course the Navy has heads aboard their ships, but that is another subject altogether.
Heat	Wild dogs and bowlers go out in the noonday sun. The official cut-off temperature is 35 degrees Celsius when play is resumed in the bar.

Heat...

Hemline...

Hemline	Something full of excitement. You don't know where it is. It varies almost daily like the value of the dollar, varying according to the whims of fashion. Ah, but not with bowls: the rule says hemlines must not go above 38 centimetres from the ground.
Henry VIII	In 1495 he decreed: 'No one apprentice shall play at the Tenys, Closshe, Dise, Cardes, Bowles nor any unlawful game'. Yes, he understood its dangers.
Henselite	In 1930, W. D. Hensell and his son Ray produced the first one-piece plastic bowl, the Henselite, and so Australia became the world's biggest manufacturer of bowls. You might say Australia's greatest contributions to culture have been plastic bowls, Vegemite, the boomerang and the rotary clothes hoist.
Hook	A grave ailment. The only hope is to go to a clinic to be cured. There they will tell you not to let your elbow drift, not to turn your wrist on delivery, not to have your feet too far apart and to make sure your arm is absolutely parallel on the back swing. However the complaint, like smoking, is devilish hard to cure. Next up, you'll still be hooking like Ian Botham at Lord's.

I

Inclement	Charming euphemism used by club secretaries for absolutely appalling weather and play is off for the day.
Indoor Bowls	Telling the story of your play for three hours across the dinner table.

Hook...

Kitty...

J

Jack High

1. Jack is often like that.
2. 'Jack High' on television became a programme which started to out-rate murder, mayhem and even some of those kindly family shows filled with rape and incest. It was nice to discover that lawn bowls wasn't yawn bowls.

K

Kill

One kills when one belts the kitty out of the playing area. Murder is another matter. It is not prevalent at bowling clubs, even though one frequently feels like it.

Kitty

This is the jack. Or they even call it Kate. There's deep confusion over its sex. Even so it is a dear, sweet little creature whom you have been trying to cuddle up to for 25 years.

Knees

Most of us have two of them and they can be contrary items. Footballers go in the knees very early and have to be taken out and shot. Bowlers find that their knees are like old car springs, they don't bend easily. They need careful warming before action. You can always hear those knees as folk go down for their deliveries. As Nancy Mitford used to say of ladies curtseying to the Queen, 'their knees go off like pistol shots'.

L

Laughter	Something you delicately try to suppress when your opponent sends down a wrong bias.
Lawn	Yes, it is lawn bowls and the lawn at the club is so finely clipped it is like the baize of a billiard table. Indeed sometimes on a Saturday afternoon, for as long as a twentieth of a second, you get a feeling of guilt about the lawn at home which you haven't mowed for four weeks and haven't weeded since 1978.
Lead	Character who rolls the jack, lays the mat and has first bowl—on those rare occasions when he wins the toss. He is also expected to play the first brilliant draw shot. You fix up for him later.
Length	You might be short in height, short of money, short of breath, short of a gallop, short in pastry, far too short in your hem line, but if you haven't got length in bowls you are nowhere.
Lie	The correct lie is one of the great aims of the game. You get a good lie, a bad lie, even a snug lie. Actually the best lies you get in the bar, about 5.30 pm.
Lignum Vitae	A wood so dense it won't even float. It comes from Haiti and the West Indies and as far back as 1750 it has been the favoured stuff for bowls. But Lignum Vitae became hard to get, it tended to crack in excessively hot climates, and besides, who could afford it? In some of the very nicest and most superior clubs in England you still see bowls of Lignum Vitae and

Lie...

Marker...

	they claim, like Stradivarius violins, they have special qualities. But most people who play with 'woods' have never seen one.
Live Bowl	One of the half dozen who didn't go to sleep at the annual meeting.
Logo	From the Greek *logos*, meaning 'a sign' or 'reason'. Now it actually means you are deep in the hands of commerce and you have to wear a sign on your shirt that a munificent booze or tobacco company is paying for it all.
Loose End	You can have a tight end and you can have a loose end. Not to be confused with wit's end.
Luck	Dished out in unfair, unreasonable, unwarranted, unspeakable quantities, always to your opponents.

M

Male Bowler	Chauvinist who thinks he should have the best days and the best rinks, but fully approves when the females make the sandwiches, make the tea, and arrange the club socials. (*See* Female Bowler.)
Marker	Non-combatant who watches over the play, and when two woods are near equidistant from the jack, takes measurements. The marker has the right equipment, often a telescopic rod which will measure to fractions of a millimetre. For markers you pick lovable creatures who haven't had their eyesight tested since 1952.

Mat	Rectangular piece of material from which you deliver the bowl. Too small to use for prayers and too large to wipe away your tears.
Mixed Bowls	Type of team play in which you discover that one sex is not as helpless, unskilled, gentle, or loving as you once thought.
Modesty	Invariably found on the rink. It could be the last sport where players don't kiss each other or throw a fist in the air after a triumph.

N

Narrow Bowl	Sending down a bowl at too narrow an angle, so that it ends up precisely where it shouldn't be. Actually the number of narrow bowlers would be about one in fifty.
Newspapers	Daily journals which give an absurd amount of space to infinitely less popular pastimes, such as football, racing, cricket, golf, tennis . . .
Novice	One who hasn't discovered the location of the bar.
Nudge	There are various kinds of nudges. You can nudge kitty. Or you can give it a bit of a nudge in the bar. But the best kind of nudges are delicate, soft and not too aggressive.

Mixed Bowls...

Old...
8

O

Obstructing	Pinching the car when your wife's trying to get to bowls.
Old	Old bowlers never die, they just loose their bias.

P

Pace	An indecipherable, unfathomable element, which you never quite master. It depends on the wind, the moisture, the variety of grass, or how much Fred used the roller last week. Then too, the end areas where the bowlers have been walking are faster than the middle. Another imponderable is the pace of your old arm. Shouldn't have done all that gardening on Thursday.
Paddock	Of course you can 'take grass' but if you really want to give the impression that you have played for several decades you urge your number two to 'take more paddock'.
Penalty	Playing until 8.30 pm then having to buy pizza for dinner.
Pencil	You must have a pencil so that you can mark your scorecard. Ball point pen? Bowlers go through hell with ball point marks on their white gear.

Pennant	It's your dream to play pennant bowls for your club, and it is always a mystery why the selectors have not picked on your obvious merits. Meantime pennant bowls is also the darned competition which is taking up all the best rinks when you are trying to get a game.
Percentage	All the go amongst professionals. You estimate your percentage chance on every shot and so minimise your errors. With a little care you can lose by one hundred per cent.
Perfect Length	A lady's hemline must reach to no less than 38 centimetres from the ground. Of course you get away with much more if you are only 45 centimetres tall.
Pineapple	You think you are sending down what you believe is the perfect delivery and it goes off like a wayward satellite. That's a pineapple. At least with a satellite you can self-destruct.
Polish	Oh yes, there are numerous brands of polish, and you lovingly polish your bowls before setting out in the morning. Polished bowls roll better and nasty bits of stuff don't stick to them. You may not have polished your shoes since last Tuesday but always you have polished your bowls.
Positive Thinking	Remembering the BYO bag for the club party.
Post Mortem	That wonderful time when you give your spouse a blow-by-blow, end-to-end, rubber-by-rubber description of the wonderful plays you made during the afternoon. It is best to make a quick examination afterwards just to make sure spouse was listening.

Perfect Length...

Profanity...

Practice	Working on your own against an imaginary opponent. The only time you can be sure of a clean, honest victory.
Profanity	Nice term for oaths and four-letter words. In competition, try to use phrases that can't be lip read on television.
Professionals	There have been professionals in bowls only since 1980. Now a tiny band of famous bowlers travel the world in the manner of pro golfers and tennis players. They wouldn't earn enough to pay McEnroe's elocution lessons.
Pudding	Official measure of power. Most common definition: 'Too much pudding, you _ _ _ _ _ _ _ idiot.'

Q

Quiet	Bowls is a sedate game. There are no raucous noises from the gallery as in baseball, football or (shudder) tennis. When the bowler crouches to make a delivery there is a feeling of absolute tension. Even the birds stop chirping. The only noise you should hear is the creaking of bones and the stretching of over-worked cotton.

Quiet...
!
CRACK!

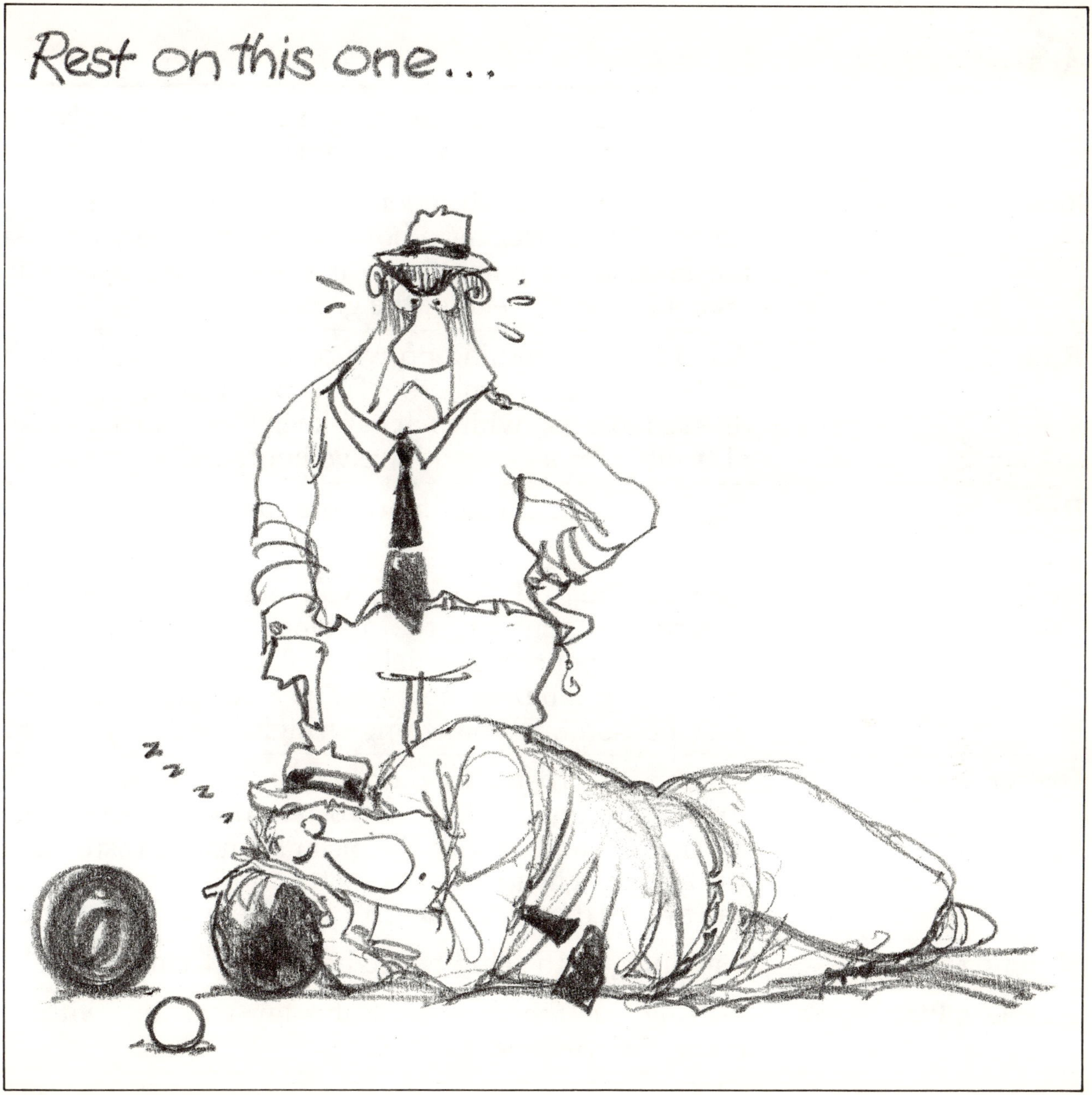
Rest on this one...

R

Rain	Disagreeable precipitation which should only be allowed between 9 pm and 8 am.
Rest on this One	You will get this instruction from your skip. He naively expects you to deliver a bowl to rest precisely against the bowl he is pointing at. It doesn't mean you can take a kip on the end of the green.
Rink	An area for trundling brown or black biased balls. It encloses large numbers of assorted people, nicely dressed in clean whites. It can keep them quiet and out of trouble for as long as twelve hours a day.
Rink Lawyer	The b _ _ _ _ _ _ who knows the rules better than you do.
Roll	Please! You roll the jack, you don't throw it. The experts say you vary the distance by lengthening or shortening your step at delivery. After contending with bias isn't it amazing how hard it is to throw . . . I beg your pardon, *roll* something straight?
Roster	There's the roster to pick up Beryl, Sylvia, Mardi, Joan, Judy and Doris, the roster to make the sandwiches, tea and provide the biscuits and the roster later for bridge. Then there's a roster to fill for those who can't make the roster. Rosters are a very serious matter.
Running Shot	Galloping to the club house before they cut off lunch.
Ruthless Play	Getting out the door on Saturday morning without doing the washing-up.

Rink Lawyer...

Shot Bowl...

S

Salt and Pepper	Devices placed on dinner tables for use when explaining tactics.
Scoring	Unselfishly assisting with the club's finances by running up the best bar bill.
Selector	Noble creature who selects the team for inter-club competition. He has only four friends.
Shoot from the Hip	One shoots from the hip when one's knees are not bending with the old flexibility. It is difficult to achieve the same accuracy as Matt Dillon.
Shot Bowl	Did we tell you that it is a crazy game? You'd think a shot bowl was one that was crook, finished. The shot bowl is one that right now is nearest to the jack.
Sin	John Aylmer (1521–1594), Bishop of London, thought it no sin to play bowls at Fulham Palace on Sunday afternoons. We think it sound to give you this precedent otherwise the sin committed around the suburbs on Sundays would be the biggest thing since the burning of Gomorrah.
Singles	Lonely non-bowlers who do all the cooking and housework.
Sir Francis Drake	1. Knew the absolute importance of the game. As the Spanish Armada approached Plymouth Hoe he uttered the immortal words: 'There is plenty of time to win the game and beat the Spaniards too'.

	(Just try putting over that excuse when you are two hours overdue.) 2. As Freddie Trueman once said, he was the last bowler to be knighted.
Skip	Man in charge of a team that always thinks it knows better than he does. (*See* Team.)
Skittles	Derisive term, handy to have up your sleeve when you have been blasted into a ditch. 'Are you good at skittles old chap?'
Smoking	It's the one sport where they will let you smoke as you play. The famous English professional David Bryant never has a pipe out of his mouth. A good smoke screen of old, ripe, cured Virginia is right for at least ten points.
Sponsor	Kindly conglomerate, firm, tobacco company or bank which will give you money provided you give back twice as much in return.
Spring	A much over-rated season, good for daffodils, tulips, freesias and the planting of lettuce and tomatoes, but not much else. The weather is too unreliable, too quixotic, too windy, but in areas laughably called temperate, there is one compensation—it is the start of the bowling season.
Sprinkler	Irrigation device designed to cast water directly across the path to the club house.
Stance	Absolutely fundamental. Before you take off your feet must be evenly balanced on the mat. This stance is nothing to some of the stances you take in the bar. They tend to be conservative.

Smoking...

Sympathy...

Stockings	Of course they are compulsory. Ladies are required also to wear long slips and to have a respectable hem length. Such things assist in the unerring concentration of male bowlers.
Straight	The charm is this—the darned thing is so mysterious. It only starts to curve when it slows down. Pure physics actually. $F=M \times V^2$ Force equals mass by velocity squared. Just do a quick calculation on your computer before you go down and you can't go wrong.
Stumpy Paddock	Rink which you feel does not have the superb, horizontal smoothness suited to your talents.
Summer	Divine time when the cicadas are screeching, when peaches, strawberries and nectarines are at their juiciest, when chrysanthemums and dahlias are in bloom. Ah, but best of all, when the rinks are hard and fast for good bowling, and, heaven be blessed, with daylight saving, it doesn't get too dark to see kitty until 9 pm.
Sweet Delivery	When the lady next door drives you to the club.
Sympathy	A beautiful emotion that you have for your opponent in the club house . . . after he's lost.
Synthetic	Very popular in the United States. Comes in a number of charming colours. Instead of using a mower and a roller you use a vacuum cleaner. Hard wearing, low maintenance cost, it is inevitably the surface of the future. Pity! The stuff God made was very nice, kind to the feet and smelt divinely when freshly cut.

Synthetic...

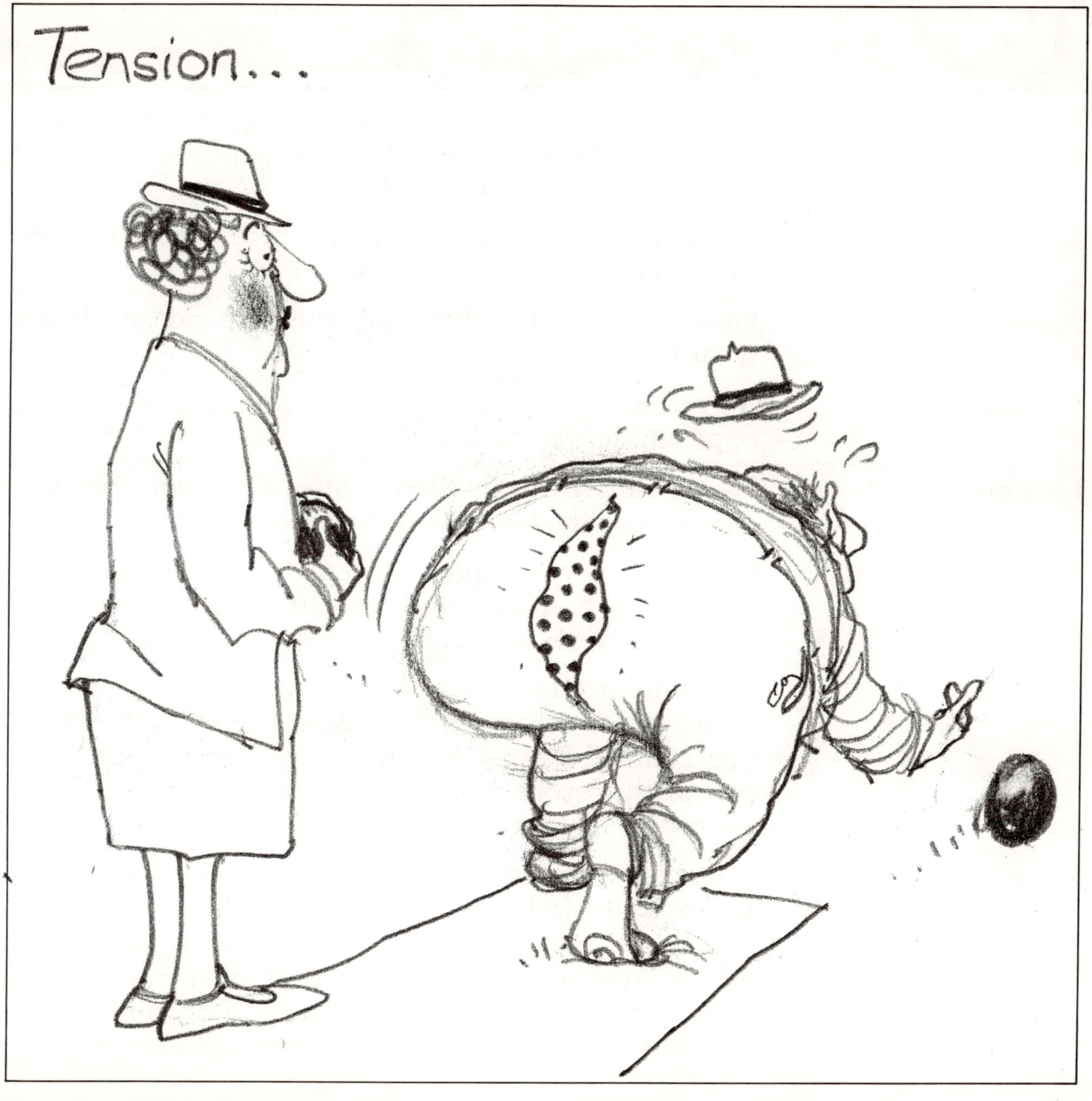
Tension...

T

Tactics	Hanging back a little and not buying the first round when the ladies order all those fancy drinks like Pimms, Gin, Lime and Soda, Whisky and Dry.
Tea	Break taken in mid-afternoon where you get sweet cake and granite-hard scones.
Team	Group of players who think the skip doesn't know what he's doing. (*See* Skip.)
Temperament	Refraining from giving a raspberry when your opponent has a toucher.
Tension	There is more of this than in any other sport, particularly across the back of the trousers.
Third	Usually the vice-captain of the team. Has to show admirable humility and try to keep quiet when obviously the skip doesn't know what he's doing.
Thirteen	Normally it takes 13 seconds, give or take a second, for a bowl to roll down the green. It is a length of time that can feel like an eternity, particularly if you have put on the wrong bias and it is heading over yonder towards the ladies' washroom.
Tiger Balm	A magic potion to remove the aches is essential. Some go for Tiger Balm invented by the Chinese herbalist Aw Chu King in the dim past. Others go for goanna oil, the Australian bush recipe, said to cure everything from arthritis to the Black Death. The smell is so superbly aromatic it can also cure you of opponents.

Tiger Balm...

Tight Play	Total abstention is absolutely necessary. W. C. Fields always gave the advice: Never drink anything stronger than gin before breakfast.
Tilt	The game is beautifully crafted so that almost everything means something else. When you tilt it means you want to go straight.
Top Spin	The feeling you get when you beat the club champion.
Toucher	One who touches kitty, and if one is wise that is all one touches.
Tours	These are all the rage. Jet Terrific Tours arranges bowling holidays. It can be just a week-end trip down the coast, or the grand bowling tour of Europe and the East. You don't have to waste your time looking at the Tower of London, the Louvre, the Vatican, the Leaning Tower of Pisa, the Taj Mahal or the great cathedrals. Much better . . . you bowl every day.
Training	In the old days training for bowls was serious stuff like going to bed at 9 pm on the day before a match, not wearing out your muscles cleaning windows or floor sweeping and eating steak and eggs for breakfast. Now they are dead serious; they expect you to diet and do exercises. Good grief, there are competitors who do yoga, aerobics, walk five kilometres a day and (shudder) even jog.
Trophies	Easily tarnished dust-gathering objects, unsuitable even for holding flowers, that other people get to put on their TV sets.

Training...

Turf...

Turf	There was a time when all grass was seeded. Terribly old-fashioned. Now you buy your grass by the square metre and it comes in a roll like the best Axminster. Darned stuff still has to be cut and rolled three times a week. One bowling green is more worry than a set of quintuplets.
Two (Second)	He gets the job at number two because they can't think of any other place to put him. He keeps the scorecard and the board up to date. Then when the lead has failed utterly in his job it is the second who is expected to play the perfect draw shot. It is almost as important as being a wife.

U

Umpire	Settles all fights and makes the decision when to retire at the coming of the flood.
Unbeatable Bowl	Bowl which rests on top of the jack in the ditch. It's the sort of situation you can get into when arguing with your wife.
Unfit	When you pant while working the club pinball machines.
Upmanship	• Tell him you are a newcomer and have played only twice before. He'll know you are a liar and that will un-nerve him.

Umpire...

Venom...

- Tell him there's a soft wet patch half way down the track. Even if it isn't there it will un-nerve him.
- Cough as he makes his delivery.
- Get all his friends to wave from the other end.
- As he goes down to make his delivery tell him his fly's undone.

V

Venom

It looks such a nice, kindly game played by gentle people dressed like so many curates and deaconesses. That's until one of them is trapped, shut out, in an unwinnable position. That's when he, and, oh yes, she, decides to send down a real belter. Venom could well be an understatement.

W

Weed

There are those who say you should never disparage a weed. It is all a matter of environment. A weed could be some beautiful flower or life-giving herb in disguise. But a weed on a bowling green is like finding a wart on

	the nose of Elizabeth Taylor. It is a matter of immense consternation. You send for beauticians and surgeons — horticultural and otherwise.
Weight	Something you put in to give the wood pace. It is not lacking at bowling clubs. Indeed some of it is awesome, particularly when it bends over.
Wick	You don't ricochet, you don't bounce, you don't even cannon off the cush. The correct term is you 'wick off' another bowl and it is known as the 'wick shot'.
Wind	A very curious element. It is never where you want it. The flags up on the club house indicate that it is coming from the West while down on the green it is gusting from the East. You will find it is absolutely incredible how the wind always assists your opponent.
Winter	A time of the year when you get yourself to a place where they are still playing bowls.
Wobble	The worst thing you can do is to deliver a wood so that it has wobble. Wobble isn't much good when you come through the door at 9 pm either.
Wood	The first bowls were made out of stone, then came wood, oak, Lignum Vitae, rubber, plastic, composition moulded from Phenol formaldehyde. You rarely see wood these times, but the bowl always is still referred to lovingly as the 'wood'. It sounds nicer than Phenol formaldehyde.
Work	Something which at your age should be carefully avoided. It is said to cause stress and interferes absolutely with your bowling day.

Weight...

Wrong Bias...

Wrest This is the shot you play when your opponent's bowl is the target. It is a charming, bowlerish term for saying you are going to knock the blighter out of your way.

Wrong Bias She doesn't know a Henselite from a billiard ball, but she has rather a good end, she throws a splendid curve, and from the right angle her back swing has much to recommend. Your spouse thinks partnership with her is remarkably wrong bias.

X

X It happens every day. The skip says, right here, he wants your wood right on that spot. You are blocked except for a gap three centimetres wide. It's blowing a gale, you are using an instrument that curves like a gasometer, yet you are expected to place it on X. Who says it's a game without skill?

Y

Yard On Getting into the lunch queue before all the rest.

Young You are seeing lots of them in bowls now, young characters, no grey hairs, beautiful reflexes, backs that don't hurt, 20–20 vision. Thank God, it still takes twenty years to learn some of the things *you* know.

X...
SHOTS
ENDS
SHOTS

Z

Zero	You had incredible bad luck, didn't get a decent lie all day, the wind always was working against you, and who could play on that rink anyway? Zero was your score against the club champion.
Zing	The zip which you miss when you were a young bowler of eighty-five.